teach me about

Travel

Copyright © Joy Berry, 2022
Originally Published, 1986

All rights are reserved.

No part of this book can be duplicated or used without the prior written permission of the copyright owner, except for the use of brief quotations from the book.

For inquiries or permission requests contact the publisher.

Published by Joy Berry Enterprises
www.joyberryenterprises.com

teach me about

Travel

By JOY BERRY

Illustrated by Bartholomew

Joy Berry Enterprises

I get ready to go.

I get dressed.

I go to the bathroom.

I get the things

I want to take with me.

I take my sweater or jacket.

I take my favorite blanket or toy.

I take something to do.

I do not want my hands or feet

to get closed in the car door.

I am careful

when I get into the car.

I keep my hands and feet

away from the door.

I do not want to get hurt.

I get into my car seat.

I fasten my safety belt.

I stay in my car seat

while I am in the car.

I do not want my hands

to get caught in the window.

I do not roll the window

up or down.

I do not want to fall out of the car.

I do not unlock the car door.

I do not touch the door handle.

I do not get out of the car

until it is parked.

I do not want the car to crash.

The person driving the car must think about driving.

I do nothing that would bother the person driving the car.

I do not want to lose anything.

I do not throw anything

out of the car window.

I do not want to get lost.

I do not go anywhere by myself.

I always stay with the person

who is taking care of me.

Sometimes I ride in a shopping cart.

I do not want to fall out of the cart.

I sit down in the shopping cart.

I do not want anything to fall on me.

I do not reach for things that are outside the **shopping cart.**

Sometimes I eat away from home.

I sit in a high chair or

booster chair.

I do not want to fall.

I sit carefully in the chair.

Sometimes I sleep away from home.

I miss my house.

I miss my bed.

I remember that I will be home soon.

Then I do not feel so bad.

It is fun to go away.

It is also fun to come back home.

I am careful

so I can come back home safely.

helpful hints for parents about
Traveling

Dear Parents:

The purpose of this book is—
- to show children how to prepare for travel, and
- to teach children what they need to do to remain safe and well while they are traveling.

You can best implement the purpose of this book by—
- reading it to your child, and
- reading the following *Helpful Hints* and using them whenever applicable.

TRAVEL SAFETY

Safety procedures for travel include:
- Provide a safety-tested and approved car seat for your child.
- Have your baby's car seat ready for the first ride home from the hospital.
- Pad and cover your car seat and infant carrier with an absorbent material such as terry cloth.
- Always use the restraining belts in both car seats and infant carriers.
- Never leave your child unattended in a car seat or infant carrier.

TRAVELING SUPPLIES

Suggested items to keep in your car:
- A washable or disposable changing surface. Plastic garbage bags work well and can be used for diaper disposal.
- Premoistened towelettes for easy cleanup.
- Ointment or powder for diaper rash.
- A minimum of two disposable diapers.
- Plastic bags for used diapers.
- Eating and drinking utensils, including a plastic baby bottle, spoon, and cup.
- A bib.
- Sealed containers of fruit juice and baby food.
- Protective clothing such as a sweater, a jacket, a warm hat, or a sun hat.
- A full change of clothing.

- One or more baby blankets.
- Small toys and security objects.

Keep these items in a box or bag and replace them as they are used.

Suggested medical supplies to take when you travel with your child:

- vitamins
- thermometer
- baby aspirin
- diaper rash ointment
- medicine for diarrhea
- antihistamines for colds or allergies
- glycerin suppositories for constipation
- sunscreen lotion
- vital information such as your doctor's phone number, medical insurance card or number, and a health information book.

All medications should be in child-proof containers. Keep important medications with you. Do not put them in baggage that might be lost or stolen.

EQUIPMENT NEEDED AWAY FROM HOME

Take only what you and your child will need when you travel. Many of the necessities can be borrowed or rented when you reach your destination. You may want to call ahead to reserve them.

Here are some items your child will most likely need while away from home:
- A car seat.
- A portable potty. This is especially good for long car trips.
- A bed.
- A playpen. This can also be used as a bed.
- A standard or portable highchair. A portable one can be attached to a table top. (Most restaurants supply highchairs.)
- A walker. This can be used in place of a highchair.
- A stroller.
- An infant seat.
- A baby carrier.

When your child sleeps away from home, you can create an instant bed from one of the following:
- A dresser drawer that has been removed from the dresser (for small infants only).
- Covered foam padding.
- A playpen mat.
- An inflatable wading pool. (This can also be used as a bathtub or playpen.)

These beds should be placed on the floor in an area that is safe and free of drafts. Be sure to provide enough padding to make the bed comfortable.

FOOD AND BEVERAGES FOR TRAVEL

Bottles

Procedures for keeping bottles cold:
- Put six bottles in a six-pack container and place the container in a six-pack ice chest.
- Wrap the bottle in a small towel or diaper, then pack it in ice cubes in a sealable plastic bag.

Procedures for warming bottles and keeping them warm:
- Fill a plastic container with hot water and place the bottle in the water. The contents should be warm in three to six minutes.
- Run the hot tap water over the bottle until the contents are warm.
- Wrap the warm bottle in a dry washcloth. Place it in an empty tennis ball can and snap on the plastic lid.

Beverages

Here are some suggestions for preparing beverages for travel:
- Premeasure powdered formula and put it into a sealable plastic bag. Add warm water from a Thermos bottle when your baby is ready to eat.
- Prewarm canned formula and carry it in a Thermos bottle.
- Carry a large Thermos jug of cold water and plastic cups with handles. Water from home is less likely to cause digestive problems.
- Add premeasured servings of hot cocoa mix to hot water from a a Thermos bottle when traveling in cold weather.
- Freeze sealed containers of juice before your trip. Allow the beverages to defrost en route.

- A Thermos bottle of fruit juice or water with an opening for a straw will work well for your child over 18 months.

Food

Some good snack choices for children two and older:
- bagels
- bagged trail mix
- boxed or bagged raisins
- cheese chunks
- cut up raw vegetables
- fruit leathers
- grapes
- rice cakes
- unsalted popcorn

TRAVEL ENTERTAINMENT

Here are some suggestions for entertaining children while they are traveling:
- Small soft dolls, hand or finger puppets, and small people figures are good company in a car seat.
- A toy with a suction-cup base is great for long restaurant waits in a high chair.
- Inflatable toys pack easily and provide full-size fun at your destination.

- A small cassette recorder with a supply of favorite tapes and accompanying books invite participation. Carry a blank tape to record your child's travelogue.
- For very young children, tie each toy to their car seat with elastic. This will enable them to choose or retrieve their toys without your help.
- Keep a basket of toys at the home of a frequently visited relative or friend. This saves transporting the toys back and forth and makes them seem special to your child.

TRAVELING TO THE BEACH

Here are some ideas for making a beach outing successful:
- Take plenty of water for both drinking and rinsing off sand.
- Protect your child from the sun with light clothing, a water-repellent sunscreen, a wide-brimmed hat, and an umbrella or sun shade.
- Put jar lids under the legs of the playpen to keep it from sinking into the sand.
- Carry your child's toys in a mesh bag. Then rinse the bag and the toys in water before you leave the beach.

www.ingramcontent.com/pod-product-compliance
Lightning Source LLC
Chambersburg PA
CBHW081410070526
44583CB00020B/2757